To Market, To Market

The
Child's
World®

Distributed by The Child's World®
1980 Lookout Drive • Mankato, MN 56003-1705
800-599-READ • www.childsworld.com

Acknowledgments
The Child's World®: Mary Berendes, Publishing Director
The Design Lab: Kathleen Petelinsek, Design and Page Production

Library of Congress Cataloging-in-Publication Data
Newman, Winifred Barnum.
  To market, to market / illustrated by Winifred Barnum-Newman.
     p. cm.
  Summary: A retelling of the Mother Goose verse, with end notes listing the
benefits of nursery rhymes.
  ISBN 978-1-60253-532-9 (library bound : alk. paper)
  1. Nursery rhymes. 2. Children's poetry. [1. Nursery rhymes.] I. Mother
Goose. II. Title.
 PZ8.3.N4664To 2010
 398.8–dc22   2010015202

Printed in the United States of America in Mankato, Minnesota.
July 2010
F11538

ILLUSTRATED BY WINIFRED BARNUM-NEWMAN

To market, to market,
to buy a fat pig.

To MARKET

PIES PLUM BUNS pigs hogs

2 For 5¢

Home again,
home again,

6

jiggety-jig.

To market, to market,
to buy a fat hog.

PIES PLUM BUNS pigs·hogs

2 For 5¢

9

Home again,
home again,

jiggety-jog.

To market, to market,
to buy a plum bun.

Home again, home again,
market is done.

POEM ACTIVITY

To market, to market, to buy a fat pig.
**Turn to your right and march in place. Clap your
hands four times while marching.**

Home again, home again, jiggety-jig.
Face the front again and do a silly dance.

To market, to market, to buy a fat hog.
**Turn to your left and march in place. Clap your
hands four times while marching.**

Home again, home again, jiggety-jog.
Face the front again and do an even sillier dance.

To market, to market, to buy a plum bun.
**Continue facing the front and march in place.
Rub your tummy in circles.**

Home again, home again, market is done.
Clap two times and take a bow.

BENEFITS OF CHILDREN'S POEMS AND SONGS

Children's poems and songs are more than just a fun way to pass the time. They are a rich source of intellectual, emotional, and physical development for a young child. Here are some of their benefits:

* Learning the words and activities builds the child's self-confidence—"I can do it all by myself!"

* The repetitious movements build coordination and motor skills.

* The close physical interaction between adult and child reinforces both physical and emotional bonding.

* In a context of "fun," the child learns the art of listening in order to learn.

* Learning the words expands the child's vocabulary. He or she learns the names of objects and actions that are both familiar and new.

* Repeating the words helps develop the child's memory.

* Learning the words is an important step toward learning to read.

* Reciting the words gives the child a grasp of English grammar and how it works. This enhances the development of language skills.

* The rhythms and rhyming patterns sharpen listening skills and teach the child how poetry works. Eventually the child learns to put together his or her own simple rhyming words— "I made a poem!"

15

ABOUT THE ILLUSTRATOR

Winifred Barnum-Newman is a writer, poet, painter, sculptor, illustrator, and designer. She is internationally recognized as an author and illustrator of her own books as well as an illustrator of others' works. She has also written newspaper articles and poetry.

In addition to being in her studio, Winifred enjoys playing the piano and guitar, singing, and she especially loves playing with her children and grandchildren.